I Keep Getting Mad

by Isaiah W. Thompson

ISBN-13:978-1976177200

ISBN-10:1976177200

Thanks to everyone who supported my efforts! Special thanks to God who I love with all my heart. Dad (Cleve Thompson), Mom (Cher-Rhonda Woodard-Lynk), Papa (Martin Woodard, My Nana (Annie and Martin Woodard), My Grandma (Evie Thompson). My Teachers at Milwaukee College Prep (36th Street Campus), My Pastor John McVicker and Youth Director, Mrs. Marilynn McVicker. Thank you to all my cousins, friends, aunts and uncles. I love all of you!

I am the captain of my own ship! I am on the road less traveled to college and beyond!

My name is Kurt.
I am in the 1st grade. I am very smart.
My parents love me a lot and they want
me to do good at school, but sometimes
I have bad days. I get mad when I have
bad days.

Our days are quite busy. We do math, spelling, and a lot of reading.

Then my teacher sends me to sit by myself. I don't like sitting by myself so I get mad.

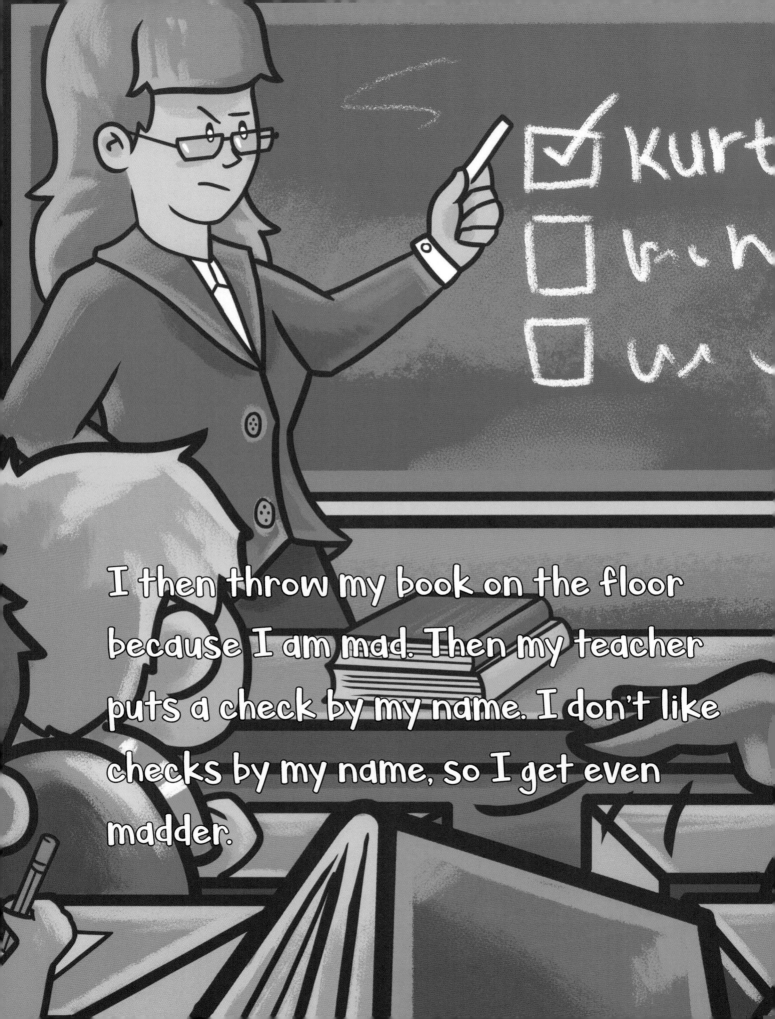

I then throw my book on the floor because I am mad. Then my teacher puts a check by my name. I don't like checks by my name, so I get even madder.

Now my teacher gives me a red card and sends me to talk with the principal. I really hate red cards. Now I am really mad!

I am still mad because I have to go to the principal's office.

My principal talks to me and tell me about all of the things that I can do, so that I won't get checks and red cards. He tells me that when I am disruptive my teacher can't teach the class so we can be smart.

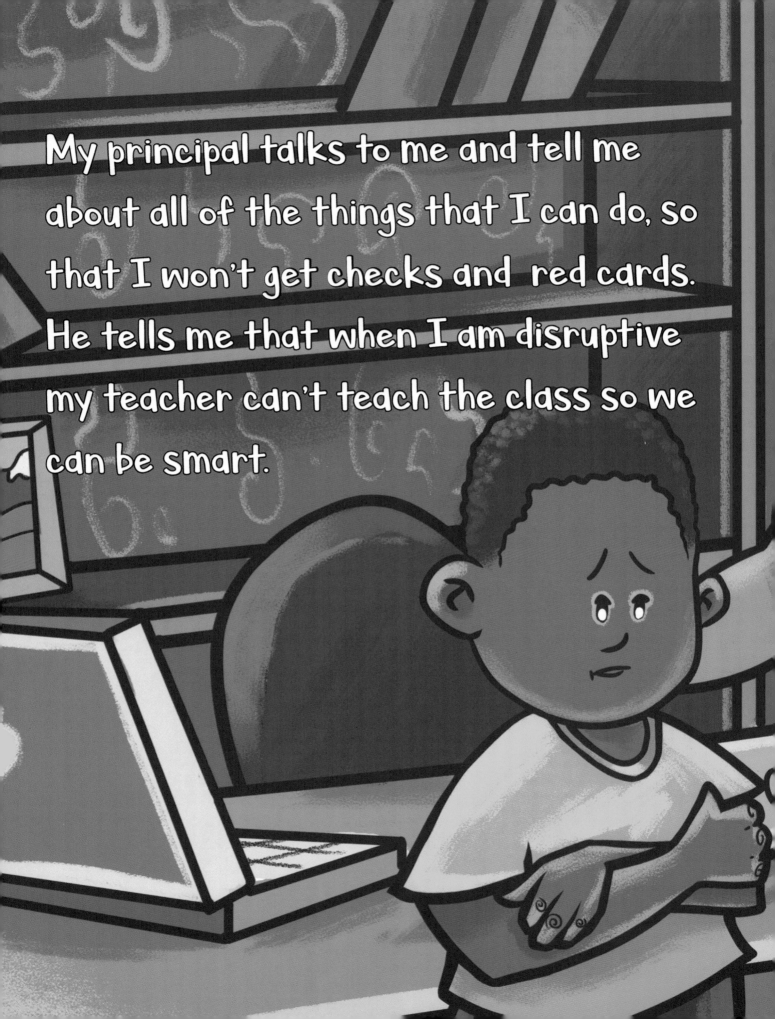

He asks me what I want to be when I grow up. I tell him that I want to be a race car driver like Dale Earnhardt. I want to drive really fast! He tells me that first I have to be very smart and listen to my teacher, so that I can grow up to be a really fast race car driver!

From now on I am going to make sure that I am on my best behavior forever! So, one day I can become a great race car driver!

Made in the USA
Columbia, SC
27 January 2018